TEXT YOU

Change Your Life
One Text at a Time

Kellie Acosta

Website: www.TextYouBook.com
Blog: www.TextYou.me

Also by Kellie Acosta
Text You for Teens (forthcoming 2012)

Published by Born Global Publishing, Atlanta, Georgia

Text You is a trademark of Kellie Acosta and is under license.

Ordering Information
Special discounts are available on quantity purchases by corporations, associations, and others.

For details, contact:
Sales@BornGlobalPublishing.com

Library of Congress Cataloging-in-Publication Data
Acosta, Kellie
Text you: change your life one text at a time

ISBN: 978-0-615-50743-9 (pbk.)
LCCN: 2011917139
Printed in the United States of America

Cover Design: David Litwin
Copyediting: Marj Hahne

Your playing small does not serve the world.

Nelson Mandela

Table of Contents

Introduction

You've probably picked up this book because either you were intrigued by the title or you encountered someone who was excited about *Text You* and the power of texting yourself. At this point, you may be asking yourself, "What is this book actually going to do for me?"

The answer is simple: *Text You* is going to change your life—one text at a time.

Before I created *Text You*, just like you, I wanted solutions. I'd recently become an empty nester, been downsized, returned to school to get a bachelor's degree, had medical issues, and been dumped by my significant other.

Through that difficult time, I discovered the simple strategy of texting myself. As conditions shifted—profoundly, sometimes immediately—I began experimenting with all the different ways that texting myself could support me through life's daily struggles. And it worked! So, of course, I had to share Text You with others.

In July 2010, I launched a blog at www.TextYou.me. The site has thousands of followers, many of whom have written to tell their stories—how pulling out their cell phone during a "mini crisis" and texting themselves an encouraging message transformed their life.

Text You: your personal cheerleading squad plus state-of-the-art problem solver. This concept may be simple, but the practices in this book will change the way you navigate life—and change your life forever.

Text You flows easily so that you can read it quickly and apply its principles and practices right away.

First I walk you through how Text You works; then I show you where it can fit into your daily life, for example: setting goals, asking for what you want, and decluttering your home.

I truly thank you for choosing *Text You: Change Your Life One Text at a Time*, and for being open to your new life and the limitless opportunities that lie ahead of you.

Make Text You a habit and you'll see extraordinary changes in your life: more organization, less complication, new doors opening, a sustainable feeling of control right at your fingertips.

Text You is such an easy concept to grasp. Have your cell phone handy, and brew yourself a cup of Text You coffee: 16 ounces of dark roast with cream and pure maple syrup.

If you're reading the soft cover version of *Text You*, please pass your copy on to a friend when you finish, and encourage them to do the same. Let's spread this simple uplifting idea to as many people as possible!

im-passe *noun* \\\'**im͵pas**\

a: a predicament affording no obvious escape
b: deadlock

Bypass Your Impasse

Texting has irreversibly changed the world we live in. Look anywhere and someone is either sending or receiving a text message.

Text You has seized upon this energy with a fun and wonderful way to shift your life simply by texting yourself. Texting has become second nature for many of us; when we press "SEND," we know that we're enhancing the receiver's life.

It's time to enhance *your* life. Just one text to yourself—like an encouraging word spoken at the right time—can empower you in astronomical ways.

You may recall your first public performance—a school play, a piano recital—and the battle inside your head when you looked out into the audience:

"Why is she in the front row?" How did you get picked for this role anyway? You're so stupid."

"I just wanted people to think I'm smart and brave."

"You're a mouse. You should just run."

"I can do this."

"You don't have it in you."

"I'm here, aren't I? They wouldn't have put me here if they didn't think I could do it. Just one word of encouragement, please? Someone? Anyone?"

"It's all right. You're going to do great!"

Text You shows you how to harness the power of a positive statement. Press "SEND" to vanquish the negative voices in your head, to clear the way for encouragement, prosperity, ease, and peace of mind.

Although Text You draws from the Law of Attraction, it isn't an absolute science. Law of Attraction practitioners recommend affirmative statements of intent, whereas Text You works as long as the expression of a want or need is specific and positive, because that simple articulation in writing unifies your thoughts such that your subconscious and the Universe can respond congruously with the message.

More immediately, you bypass your impasse: you quickly and easily move on from the concern at hand, trusting that it will be handled in its own time, and concentrate on the people and projects in your life.

The 3 Don'ts of Text You:

1. Don't Text You while driving.
2. Don't Text You at the table while dining with others.
3. Don't Text You while on a date.

People with passion can change the world for better.

Steve Jobs

Who Qualifies to Be a "Text Youser"?

Anyone who sends Text You messages
for the sole purpose of
becoming a better person and
adding value to the world around them.

When the student is ready, the master appears.

Buddhist Proverb

How to Text You

Every minute of every day, people around the world send encouraging text messages to others. I'll bet you, too, champion your friends and family this way, but what about yourself?

Even if you're new to texting, Text You will be a snap.

3 Easy Steps to Set Up Your Own Text You:

1. Put your name and cell-phone number in your contact list on your cell phone.

2. Pull up your name and write "[your name], your life is about to change for all the right reasons."

3. Press "SEND" and watch what happens next…

Your cell phone's particular texting instructions can be found in your user's manual or online by searching your phone make and model number. A veteran texter can help you, too!

What the mind of man can conceive and believe,
it can achieve.

Napoleon Hill, *Think and Grow Rich*

Text You Uses the Law of Attraction

The Law of Attraction rests on these metaphysical principles:

- If you think positively and believe you will be successful, you will acquire success.

- If you think negatively and believe you are doomed to failure, you will fail.

   To summarize, in Henry Ford's words: "Whether you think that you can, or that you can't, you are usually right." And look what he created!

You create the world you live in. Sure, there are things you can't control—the company you work for shuts down, a rainstorm floods your basement, your spouse and your kids have desires independent of your own—but you get to choose how to respond to everything that happens in your life and in the world. With the right attitude, you can truly make lemonade out of lemons. Consider Text You your attitude adjuster!

Technology + Ideology = Text You = A New You

People commonly misconceive the Law of Attraction as a mental process, with no action: *If I think about a red Maserati and envision a red Maserati in my driveway and feel how it feels to drive a red Maserati, it will materialize pronto, thanks to the abundant and generous Universe.*

Action is the loudest announcement to the Universe of our intention. In the "New Age," we seem to have forgotten this timeless wisdom: *You reap what you sow. You must give to get.*

So…

- If you want love, you must be loving.

- If you want money, you must exchange something for it.

- If you want friends, you must be a friend.

Makes sense, right? And the first action, perhaps, is writing down what you want. Remember, Text You works when the language is specific and positive. Texting "I don't want to get a speeding ticket on my trip" puts the focus entirely on the consequence of driving too fast. A more constructive text is "I arrive safely and early at my hotel."

Text You will help you attract the love, the money, the friends—and whatever else you want—the simplest way possible.

In a world of ever-increasing flux and instability, it's easy to feel powerless and out of control. It's easy to think we can't possibly make a difference or effect change. But only a small percentage of what happens out in the world directly influences our day-to-day life; how we react to that external world is what creates our present and future.

By shifting your internal world, Text You puts the power and control over your life back into—and in!—your own hands.

If a negative thought persists during the day:

Text You a positive message.

A positive message will divert your attention from your negative thinking to your anticipation of receiving what you want, while alerting your subconscious to work on resolving that thought.

Things turn out best for the people who make the best out of the way things turn out.

Art Linkletter

You Say "I Was Dumped" Like It's a Bad Thing

Breakups can be pretty bad—worse when you're the one being dumped. But, looking back, mine were among the best things to happen to me.

When we're grieving a breakup, it's hardly comforting to be told that all the bad things that happen in our life are meant to teach us something, to grow us up, to help us better know ourselves. I'll share how one breakup, in particular, crystallized that belief for me.

Text You was born when it occurred to me, while writing a positive text message to someone who'd just broken up with me, that I was crazy.

I was trying to put my own life back together, yet was sending reassuring and encouraging messages to my ex. Huh?!

My ex: "This breakup is so hard on me."
Me: "You'll do just great."
My ex: "I'm not handling this well."
Me: "Things will be better tomorrow."
My ex: "My life is in shambles."
Me: "Take it one step at a time."

After a couple of weeks of this, I began to question the absence of support for *me*: Where are *my* uplifting text messages? Whose pulling *me* through this?

It was a stunning revelation: nothing like this would happen unless *I* made it happen.

After figuring out how to add my own name and cell-phone number to my contact list, I'd text myself a little reassurance—"Everything is going to be fine." "Look at all you've accomplished." "One breakup isn't the end of your world." "What great adventures lie ahead as you start over again."—anytime I'd head-dive into "woe is me" thinking.

Writing and reading the supportive message, I'd immediately feel better.

It was a little awkward at first. I even began thinking of myself in the third person. What would I say to my best friend—me!—in this situation?

The results were unbelievable. I made it a practice to text myself a couple of times a week. For a while, I kept it to myself because I thought people would think I was crazy or, worse, self-centered. When I shared the technique with close friends who seemed to need a little self-motivation, they asked all sorts of questions. Most of them immediately pulled out their cell phone and added their name and number. They insisted I share Text You with others.

Soon after I launched the blog www.TextYou.me, people all over the globe were using Text You to better their lives—and the world.

All that spirits desire, spirits attain.

Kahlil Gibran

I Want It, I Text It, I Get It

Sending myself feel-good text messages was so off-the-charts amazing that I decided to use Text You to declare my needs for more tangible things.

When I returned to college as a single mom, my minimum-wage income couldn't cover all my expenses, bills, and past-due notices.

I sent myself this text: "I need $5,000."

A few hours later, my college financial adviser called to tell me they'd approved me for a student loan of $5,000.

Since it was the end of the semester and all my school expenses were paid, I could use the money for living expenses, she said. Two days later, I picked up the check.

Just to be clear, I didn't rely on magical thinking. I had taken these actions prior to that day:

1. I called my financial advisor to ask if there were any loans available to help students with personal expenses.

2. I went into the financial aid office and filled out a stack of paperwork.

And I texted myself!

The call, coming so soon after I sent the text, had to be a coincidence, I thought, but deep down I knew I had the power to manifest whatever I needed. I'd learned early about the power of belief when, at thirteen, I read Og Mandino's *The Greatest Salesman in the World*, to be followed by Napoleon Hill's *Think and Grow Rich*, Zig Zigler's *How to Get What You Want*, and Dale Carnegie's *How to Win Friends and Influence People*.

So, wanting to date again, I texted myself a complete description of the type of person I wanted to meet. Among the ten key qualities was full-time employment since I had to devote more of my time to school than to a relationship.

The next person I met, now my partner, not only qualified on all ten counts but also has worked for the same company for 28 years, leaves for work by 7:30 every morning, and comes home at 6:00. Little by little, I was realizing that texting oneself could help others just like it was helping me.

A couple of weeks after meeting my new partner, my son gave me his old iPod.

It was empty so I texted myself, "I need music for my iPod."

A few days later, I found, in my partner's CD collection, many of my favorite artists—a significant improbability because my tastes run the gamut from Janis Joplin to Harry Belafonte to The Black Eyed Peas. I downloaded over 3700 hours of music.

Since starting this experiment and making Text You a habit, I've received my bachelor's degree; I've launched my own company; I've vacationed in beautiful places like Playa del Carmen, Mexico, and Tuscany, Italy; I drive a Jaguar convertible; and I live in a beautiful house in Atlanta, Georgia, with the person of my dreams.

I tell you this not to impress you, but to impress upon you the ways in which Text You has helped me organize and achieve my goals.

A journey of a thousand miles begins with a single step.

Lao-Tzu

The Secret to Creating a Habit

Simplicity is one of the foundational principles of Text You.

If you're already in the habit of sending texts to friends and family to stay in touch, Text You will be effortless.

The secret to creating this, and any, new habit?

1) Just start.

Start. Then do it again. And again. And again.

Send yourself a text every time you initiate a text to someone else. Even a simple, positive "I can make this a better day" will head you in the best possible direction.

Just start.

Be thankful for what you have; you'll end up having more. If you concentrate on what you don't have, you will never, ever have enough.

Oprah

Do You Know How Wealthy You Really Are?

No doubt, we're living in difficult times: an unstable economy, high unemployment and divorce rates, not enough hours in a day. What helps people get through it all: an attitude of gratitude.

Each of us has something to be grateful for, even in our darkest hour. Too often, we buy in to a consumer culture that values the acquisition of more stuff: the pricier, bigger, faster—the better. Our sight, our family, a fleece blanket on the first cool night of autumn—these are our real assets. They may not be line items on a balance sheet, but they balance out our life.

Being grateful for what you already have is imperative for using Text You. To get in touch with this, consider a daily gratitude practice. Every night, record what you're grateful for in a journal, or do what my aunt does. Once in bed, she speaks aloud everything she's grateful for instead of taking a sleeping aid. Some nights, she gets further along in her list, but never does she finish it!

Sometimes we don't feel worthy of what we receive—a salary jump, a gift for no good reason, love—so we don't learn to expect abundance and appreciate the gifts when they arrive.

People who are grateful for what they receive experience greater well-being—physical, emotional, and spiritual. Believing they have enough and "the Universe will provide," they tend to be more giving. It's a beautiful cycle: the more you give, the more you receive; and the more you receive, the more you give. And so on.

The gifts you give and receive when you're grateful aren't necessarily tangible. They may be an encouraging word, a smile, or a surrendered parking spot. And who doesn't love to be appreciated? Consider this: every "Thank you," every "You're a sweetheart," every "Great job!" generates a good feeling in another that gets passed on, and on, and on—changing the world one acknowledgement at a time. Text You and launch a movement!

What three things do you have that you wouldn't
trade for anything in the world?

Text You these three things
anytime you get
stuck in negative thinking.

Alice came to a fork in the road.
"Which road do I take?" she asked.

"Where do you want to go?"
responded the Cheshire Cat.

"I don't know," Alice answered.

"Then," said the cat, "it doesn't really matter."

Lewis Carroll, *Alice in Wonderland*

Goal Setting Finally Made Fun and Easy

Write down your goals. We've all heard this good advice, but writing down our goals and regularly reading them often becomes one more piece of paper cluttering the desk, one more item on the to-do list.

Text You is a fast, convenient, reliable—and savvy!—way to declare your goals and get you out of the rabbit hole.

Without clear goals, you'll wander, like Alice, letting external forces dictate where you'll end up. Your job and income will be what someone offers you, your relationships will be with whomever you meet, and your home will be where either your job or your relationships take you.

Defining your goals allows you to align your thoughts and actions with them so that you land right where you want to be. Declaring your goals keeps you accountable to yourself, faithfully on track.

To whom do you declare your goals? Yourself and the Universe.

What do you declare? What you want.

When do you declare it? When you want it, or just before you really need it.

How do you declare it? Text You.

Text You: Your Easy Goal Tracker

1. You can write a goal anytime (e.g., waiting in line, on a coffee break, at the doctor's office).

2. You don't need pen and paper.

3. You have a complete log of all your goals (those fulfilled and those still coming to fruition).

Text You messages are SMART:

- Specific
- Measurable
- Attainable
- Realistic
- Timely

Specific: Articulate the desired outcome in precise qualitative terms.

Measureable: Articulate the desired outcome in concrete quantitative terms.

Attainable: The desired outcome is reasonably achievable or doable for any human, and for you in your lifetime.

Realistic: The desired outcome is one you're willing and able to work toward, given your resources, skills, and knowledge.

Timely: Set a target date for the desired outcome, including incremental ones for intermediate steps.

- I want at least a $2,000 raise by the first of next month.

- I want to reconnect with my high-school friend Tim this week.

- I want $90 to buy the Vibram 5 Fingers running shoes.

- I need $900 to cover next month's rent.

Now, the $90 or $900 may not magically show up on the sidewalk or in your bank account, but a friend may give you a gift card for the local sports store that they can't use, or someone may offer to pay you $900 to paint a few rooms in their house, or your boss may ask you to work late on a project over the next month and give you a bonus.

The magic lies not in getting what you want instantly, but in the quick materializing of the road to getting what you want.

The power is right at your fingertips.

What do you want?

If a rich relative said to you,

"I want to take you shopping.

You can have anything you want,"

Text You what you would want.

All you need to know in life is what you want. Then declare it.

Text You that answer—NOW!

And repeat. Practice figuring out what you want and declaring it to yourself and the Universe.

The more wants and needs you declare, the more you'll get. When you review your goals log in a couple of months, you'll be amazed by how many texts will have actualized.

We need to accept that we won't always make the right decisions, that we'll screw up royally sometimes—understanding that failure is not the opposite of success; it's part of success.

Arianna Huffington

What Is Success to You?

Is it something physical? Something you've already acquired—a beautiful apartment, a dependable car, stylish clothes?

Is it something emotional? A phone call initiated by a friend, a blossoming garden of flowers you planted in early spring, an unexpected promotion?

Or is success to you even less tangible? Being in a relationship with a person who makes you laugh? Creating a livelihood that allows you to travel when you want to? Getting to sleep in on Sundays?

There's no right or wrong answer—despite the media images and institutional messages that promote power and money and everything both can buy—as the highest ideal of success. That voice in your head—"I'll be successful when…"—probably isn't yours.

Look around you right now. Consider your typical day. Review your personal history. Think about what in your life already makes you feel successful. Take pleasure in those things. Express gratitude for them. Text You "You're all that!"

And what in your current life and history makes you feel like a failure? Let's reframe your perception: How did each of those things actually lead to success?

Express gratitude for your so-called failures.

Text You "You sure know how to turn lemons into lemonade!"

If you have debt, I'm willing to bet
that general clutter is a problem for you too.

Suze Orman

Get Your House in Order

If my home was tidier, I'd throw more parties.

If I didn't get so many emails, I'd respond more promptly to them.

Do you ever hear yourself say or think some version of these? Whether it's the house you live in, or your financial, communication, or relationship "house," the clutter has to go.

In our culture of mass consumption, we've created quite a bond with all our stuff. Piling up in the basement, garage, closet, and spare bedroom are obsolete gadgets, your "thin" clothes, back issues of magazines, your grown kids' toys. *They may come back in style. I'll get around to reading them. They hold special childhood memories.*

Add the gifts and inherited items you won't let go of because of guilt, and those roomy ugly jeans perfect for horseback riding, and... you get the point.

You may kid yourself into believing that practicality, sentimentality, or guilt is running you, but the biggest reason we don't declutter is we don't know where to start.

Text You is the solution.

With your cell phone in hand, walk through your entire home and notice which rooms or parts of rooms send you into overwhelm. A room that needs some straightening up and vacuuming may feel like a burden, but stick with the areas you want to declutter. Managing clutter can include cleaning, organizing, systematizing, rearranging, or relocating items; but here "decluttering" means getting rid of unnecessary items—stuff you don't use, need, want, or love.

As you move through your living space—including the basement, attic, garage, and car—Text You each area you want to declutter.

Next, schedule each area's decluttering with a Text You message containing:

- the day, date, and time
- the room or area
- what will keep you entertained
- a reward that will replace something old for cleaning that room—this should encourage you to give/throw something away.

Each text should look something like this:

"Thursday, 9/21, 6-9 PM - dining room - Al Green on the CD player - a new set of placemats"

After you get your home in order, tackle the other clutter in your life:

- friends and acquaintances you've outgrown
- unreturned calls and unanswered emails
- required or recommended professional development or training
- repairs to your house, car, or relationships
- neglected financial matters

Text You when a new idea comes to mind for how to create more organization and space in your life.

When you're home, just before settling into your routine, take a peek at your decluttering texts and do just *two* of them.

The space you free up, little by little, in your environment and life creates mental space: more clarity, more creativity, and more peace of mind.

Tears and fears and feeling proud
to say "I love you" right out loud.

Joni Mitchell

TEXT YOU Change Your Life – One Text at a Time

It's a Romance, Not a Loaf of Bread

You're in the checkout line at the grocery store when you remember that you need bread.

You find the bread aisle and scan the choices: buns (no), white bread (no), wheat (yes). Okay, which wheat: 9-Grains (too expensive), honey wheat (sounds healthy, delicious; it's on sale). You toss a loaf of the honey wheat into the cart.

Do you choose romantic partners this way? They look good, they'll be healthy for you, their cost-benefit ratio seems promising—so you throw them into the shopping cart of your life, then wonder why the relationship went stale after a few months?

If you aren't seeking a mate, use Text You to attract the ideal job, boss, car, home—and pass it on to your single friends!

54

Text You a list of at least
10 characteristics
you want in a partner "for life."

If someone you're romantically curious about has only six of the ten qualities, your Text You list will be a reality check of their unsuitability when you're blinded by infatuation or desperation.

Soon there will be seven billion people on this planet. If you really want a "significant other" and stay true to your Text You list, you'll attract someone whom you'll handpick—and never again settle for the most adequate person among the available options.

It takes courage to grow up and become who you really are.

e.e. cummings

15 Beneficial Ways to Text You

1. How Wonderful Life Is While You're in the World

*I hope you don't mind that I put down in words
How wonderful life is while you're in the world.*

Sir Elton John

Channel-surfing in the car, I caught the last line of Elton John's "Your Song." It occurred to me then that we each live in harmony with people who add something to our life, and tolerate or reject those who don't.

That is, those who don't follow the same god or political party we follow; those who don't look like we look, speak like we speak, love how we love; those we just don't know.

I knew that I needed to change this attitude in myself, that if I wanted to be accepted by people, I needed to be more accepting of others.

So, whenever I feel disappointed, irritated, or disgusted by someone, I chant "How wonderful life is while you're in the world" under my breath or in my mind. Immediately, people become people with good probable reasons for what they did, said, or believed, and not obstacles or inconveniences in my life.

Try it for a week: Every time someone doesn't think or act the way you want them to—speaks out against your viewpoint, cuts you off in traffic, is impatient in the checkout line, litters—say to yourself, "How wonderful life is while you're in the world." How different this world—and your life—will be if you do this simple practice. Why not start with yourself?

Text You "Life is wonderful while you're in the world."

2. Please, Sir, I Want Some More

Oliver! Oliver!
Never before has a boy wanted more.
Oliver, Oliver
Won't ask for more once he sees what's in store.

Oliver!

When the title character of *Oliver!*, in a dare among the orphan boys, draws the shortest straw and must ask the orphanage caretaker for more gruel, those six words—"Please, sir, I want some more."—alter his entire future. The ensuing chain of events lands him on the streets of London, until he's taken in by a wealthy old man who turns out to be his grandfather. Yes, Oliver lives happily ever after.

Life rarely works out the way it does in a movie, but that's not the point. What is relevant is how difficult it is for most of us to ask for more.

We're trained from the moment we begin speaking that it's rude to directly ask for something, so we stop asking in order to be accepted and fit in.

We all want more—more money, more time, more space, more patience, more love.

Text You is the technique for asking for—declaring—what you want:

"I want more money... $500 for a queen-size bed."

"I want more time... three hours to go to the movies once a week."

"I want more space... an apartment with an eat-in kitchen and a spare bedroom."

"I want more patience... to slow down and breathe before I reprimand my children."

"I want more love... long hugs from my partner."

Text You asking for more of just one thing.

3. Knock-the-Ball-out-of-the-Park Feeling

I get the greatest feeling when I'm singing. It's other-worldly. Your feet are anchored into the Earth and into this energy force that comes up through your feet and goes up the top of your head, and maybe you're holding hands with the angels or the stars, I have no idea.

Cyndi Lauper

If you've been in the stands when a ball is batted out of the park, you know there's nothing like it. It's as if time stands still. Fans cheering, the batter cruising around the bases, the team high-fiving their homerun hitter in the dugout: How do we have a life that feels like that?

Envision it.

Once you have a clear picture of what you want your life to look like, you can then move toward it, eye on the prize.

Surely you still have dreams about the life you want to live, no matter how old you are. And, having survived various life passages, you're already a pro at reinventing yourself. Text You will make this time of transition fun!

Where will you be living? Near water, in the mountains, in a high-rise, overseas? Will you have a driver and a chef, or a bike and an organic garden? Will you be surrounded by friends and family or meeting all kinds of new people? What will you be wearing, eating, doing for fun?

Live it up. To clarify your vision for your life, look through magazines for images that excite you, ask your friends how they see you, Google faraway places. *Life is not a dress rehearsal*, said British author Rose Tremain. This is it. And it's up to you to envision and execute the marvelous production that is your life.

Text You four aspects of your dream life that give you that knock-the-ball-out-of-the-park feeling.

Whenever you encounter or think of another component of your dream life, Text You a brief description of it.

You are alerting the Universe, expecting abundance, and creating an electronic record that can keep you present and accountable to your vision.

4. Lost and Found

We all lose friends… We lose them in death, to distance and over time. But even though they may be lost, hope is not. The key is to keep them in your heart, and when the time is right, you can pick up the friendship right where you left off. Even the lost find their way home when you leave the light on.

Amy Marie Walz

We find and then often lose—due to change, neglect, conflict, outgrowing each other—so many wonderful people over the course of our life:

- our best friend from childhood
- our favorite teacher
- a boss who really invested in our success
- an elderly neighbor who shared their stories with us
- a college friend who always listened without judging us

Text You the name of someone you've been thinking about but haven't seen in a long time.

By putting this person's name out to the Universe with an intention to reconnect, you'll be given the answer to how to reach them.

When that reconnection happens, let them know what they meant, and mean, to you. And tell them how wonderful life is while they're in the world! You may be pleasantly surprised by what they've been thinking about you during this time of absence.

5. I'm New Here

Never be afraid to try something new.
Remember, amateurs built the ark;
professionals built the Titanic.

Author Unknown

My first day of kickboxing class, I arrived twenty minutes early. The only one there, I sat with my hands already wrapped-up in my lap, watching the clock.

As other participants arrived, many greeted me: "Hi, are you new here?" They asked me my name and if I'd done this before. They told me their name and gave me friendly advice: "Take it slow. Pace yourself."

Within minutes, I was the new kid on the block, with a new set of friends.

During the class, several smiled encouragingly at me; afterward, some asked about how I was doing and when I'd be back. People I hadn't even met yet said, "See you next week."

If you've been wanting to try something new but hate that "new kid" awkwardness, just remember all the benefits that come with that position.

The more times you can say "I'm new here," the more dynamic, refreshing, and fulfilling your life will be.

Text You something you've been wanting to do, a class you've been wanting to take, or a place you've been wanting to visit.

6. Is It a "Get to" Day or a "Have to" Day?

I arise in the morning torn between a desire to improve the world and a desire to enjoy the world. This makes it hard to plan the day.

E.B. White

Every Saturday before Thanksgiving, we throw a huge party complete with a ping-pong tournament and a turkey shoot (well, tin cans and a BB gun).

It takes almost two months to prepare for this annual event.

One year, my partner and I took a day off together to turn the garage into the tourney room: paint the floor, throw some rugs down, hang art on the walls.

Neither one of us was moving very quickly.

At one point, I said, "Let's make this a 'get to' day instead of a 'have to' day."

Get to play on the computer without a time limit. *Get to* watch a movie in the middle of the day. *Get to* do whatever you want.

On a "have to" day, there's no getting around the to-do list. Things must get done.

At the end of a "have to" day, you feel accomplished, and your life feels more on track.

At the end of a "get to" day, you feel indulged, and your life feels invigorated.

Text You three things you think you have to do today.

If nothing seems pressing, take a "get to" day!

7. Do Something Nice for Yourself Today

Love yourself first and everything falls into line.

Lucille Ball

"Never take your taste buds for granted," Sherry advised me the first time we met in the oncologist's waiting room. She was there for a radiation treatment for her third bout of cancer. Sherry could taste only four things: mocha Kahlúa, mocha lattes from McDonald's, her own barbecue sauce (over rice or shredded chicken), and eggs.

As I got up to leave, she said, "Do something nice for yourself today. We always take time to do things for others, but we never think about doing something special for ourselves."

Sherry was right. I was super-parent for my sons, super-girlfriend for my partner, super-friend, super-daughter—but not super-Kellie for myself.

The next time I saw her, I stopped to say hello and ask her how she was doing.

"Do something nice for yourself today," she reminded me when we said goodbye. Makes you wonder if self-love is the prevention and the cure for everything that ails us. Sherry sure had enough love to go around.

What nice thing can you do for yourself when you're overwhelmed, when you need a little pampering, or just because?

- Take yourself out to lunch and a movie.
- Visit a place you enjoyed as a child.
- Take a nap.
- Tour your city like a traveler.
- Read a book outside.

Text You "Do something nice for yourself today."

8. Don't Quit

Fall seven times, stand up eight.

Japanese Proverb

Everyone on the planet has quit something. Knowing when to surrender isn't a bad idea when we're under-motivated or under-skilled, but we often give up when we lose confidence, courage, patience, or hope. Successful people aren't immune to self-doubt, fear, impatience, and hopelessness, but they likely hang on to these principles when the going gets tough:

- Give it a chance.

- Go easy on yourself.

- Get right back in there.

Distance runners are trained to "kick it in" when they get close to the finish line. Are you in the final stretch of your graduate program, your weight-loss plan, your memoir? Text You to cheer yourself to the end.

And what pursuits or dreams have you given up on before you even started? Have you always wanted to run a marathon, climb a mountain, ride a motorcycle cross-country, or play the piano? Text You to cheer yourself to begin.

If you really want to accomplish something, don't quit; but if you have quit, just start over. It's a new day.

Remember: To set yourself up to win, make sure your goals are SMART: specific, measurable, attainable, realistic, timely. "I want to lose one pound this week" is SMART—and SMARTer than "I want to lose twenty pounds over the next two months."

9. Feel Young Again

*How old would you be if you didn't know
how old you were?*

Satchel Paige

While in my mid-forties, I began anticipating the big birthday milestone still several years ahead of me.

I also began associating with that number: I'd add two years to my age when people asked; I'd feel more tired by the end of the day; I'd think about my AARP benefits.

Troubled by how quickly my forecasting became my reality, I asked people how old they were versus how old they felt.

For most, the latter number was considerably lower.

Testing out for myself that "age is just a number," I chose the minimum age I felt I could relate to—thirty-six—and observed what happened.

The results:

I feel younger.

I think younger.

I act younger.

I look younger.

Text You a winning number that represents how young you feel.

10. Do You Know the Way Back to Kindergarten?

All I really need to know about how to live and what to do and how to be I learned in kindergarten.

Robert Fulghum

One morning, while getting in the car to go to school, my grandson, Camlo, asked me if I still knew the way back to kindergarten.

That question stayed with me during the drive home and distracted me from tackling my to-do list after I got in the door.

So I sat down and recalled everything I loved about my life at five years old.

Much of it echoed a list emailed to me years ago, which I've adapted here.

Remember…

- Hide-and-seek.

- Sharing a double-stick Popsicle with a friend.

- Red Light, Green Light. Mother, May I? Red Rover.

- Hopscotch. Double Dutch. Jacks. Kickball.

- Jolly Ranchers. Bubble-gum cigarettes. Wax lips and mustaches.

- Making decisions with "Eeny, meeny, miney, mo."

- Discovering an ability on a "double-dare."

- Correcting mistakes with "Do over!"

- Staying out until the streetlights came on.

- Catching lightening bugs in a jar and poking holes in the lid.

- Jumping on the bed. Pillow fights.

- Baseball cards in bike spokes.

Who you are today is a wonderfully unique conglomeration of all your memories. Text You to return to those early days of pure joy, imagination, and innocence.

Text You one favorite memory you have of when you were five.

11. Just for the Fun of It

If you never did, you should.
These things are fun, and fun is good.

Dr. Seuss, *One Fish Two Fish Red Fish Blue Fish*

One night, friends of mine were swapping stories about jumping off their garage roofs, despite scuffed knees and stinging legs, when they were kids.

Having been raised primarily in high-rises in Chicago, I asked, "Why would anyone jump off a roof?"

"Just for the fun of it."

When was the last time you did something "just for the fun of it"?

- Buy furry boots.
- Sleep in your yard in a sleeping bag.
- Attend a college football game with your face painted in your team's colors.
- Go see a children's movie alone.

Anything that makes you think or say "I'm too old for that," or "Why would anyone do that?"—do that!

We adults get way too serious. Fun doesn't have to make sense or produce some outcome. Take a cue from a kid, or the kid you used to be— but skip the roof-jumping, okay?

Text You one thing
you want to do
just for the fun of it.

12. What Are You So Worried About, My Friend?

Worry often gives a small thing a big shadow.

Swedish Proverb

If you saw the sun today, you are lucky.

When you awoke this morning and looked out the window, did you feel lucky?

Or did you see only the problems that lie ahead of you today and take the sun for granted?

During my last month of school, I fretted so much about the final exams and projects that I almost missed the fact that it would be my last experience as a final-year student.

Once I put my worry in perspective, the last weeks became more colorful and more sentimental.

Is your worry clouding a momentous occasion in your life? Are you:

- Anxious that your wedding will go wrong?

- Scared that a project may fail?

- Nervous that your child's behavior will ruin your reputation?

- Afraid that a move to a new city will be more than you can handle right now?

Is worry your modus operandi, clouding everything and anything?

Time spent worrying is, simply, a waste of time. Worry blinds us to all the wonder, beauty, and grace around us—what makes life more than just a timeline from cradle to grave.

Text You the one thing that worries you most.

(When we see something in print, sometimes it doesn't seem so bad.)

13. Good News

The optimist sees the rose and not its thorns;
the pessimist stares at the thorns,
oblivious of the rose.

Kahlil Gibran

It takes something to be a "glass half-full" person in a culture fed 24/7 by a media that sensationalizes bad news.

We have to be our own source of good news.

We have to look for the good in everything around us.

When you see something good happening, record it with a Text You:

- Someone stops a grocery cart from hitting a car.

- Someone lets you merge into heavy traffic.

- A customer-service representative handles your complaint cheerfully, without a run-around.

- Someone gives up their seat for an elderly person.

- Someone picks up litter and deposits it in a trash can.

- The meter-checker lets you insert a quarter after the time expired.

Text You each good thing that you eyewitness.

At the end of the day, tally the good news. Try to beat it the next day. You'll be amazed by how much good is going on out there.

14. One Kind Word

We must be the change we want to see in the world.

Mahatma Gandhi

Love.

Smile.

Hope.

You.

One kind word is a little thing you can do today, and every day, to create a ripple effect that will help heal the world. One kind word can rock someone's world.

Text one word to someone who could use a word of encouragement.

Then:

15. #1 Lifesaving Text You

My cancer scare changed my life.
I'm grateful for every new, healthy day I have.
It has helped me prioritize my life.

Olivia Newton-John

When I started this project, my only intention for Text You was that it be a means for people to tune in to who they are and what they want—and to live it.

Yet, as I finished this book, I finished another chapter in my life.

I am one of the very fortunate people who scheduled and showed up for the annual mammogram that made all the difference.

It had seemed pretty routine, a nuisance even, as I had final exams coming up.

What followed was an amazing gift of life.

Late in the afternoon on the Friday before Halloween 2010, a doctor called to tell me I had breast cancer.

The week after my final exam, I underwent surgery and used the winter break to recover before the start of my final semester.

Testing out of chemotherapy, I received a radiation treatment every day for six weeks that spring.

I'm all good now.

I was lucky. Too many women aren't. Too many women haven't had a mammogram in years.

If you are one of those women, age forty or over, who has not had a mammogram in the last one to two years:

Text You Right Now
"Find the telephone number for my mammogram."

Then:

When that call has been made:

Text You
"My life is ALL GOOD.
Call made."

If you're a man who knows one of those women—as uncomfortable as it may be—text your wife, your mother, your girlfriend, your daughter:

Get a mammogram because I love you!

Then:

Text You "You're a great guy."

3 Things to Text You Every Day

I imagine that yes is the only living thing.

e.e. cummings

Yes.

The most positive word ever.

Begin your day with it. End your day with it.

Then acknowledge that you're wonderful—or whatever descriptor brings a smile to your face.

And remind yourself that, no matter what happens, you're going to do great. Because it's true.

Text You:

1. Yes.

2. You're wonderful.

3. You're going to do great.

Now, go start living the life you were born to have.

Acknowledgments

Text You is the true compilation of all the people who have gifted me with their unique grace and presence:

My mother, Susan, gave me creative independence. For as long as I can remember, she has told me I can do anything I put my mind to. When I was a child, she opened the door and sent me on my way. She continues to give me her stamp of approval and promote me loudly and lovingly. Her Facebook page is the most reliable chronicle of my successes.

My maternal grandmother, Martha, gave me reading. Every summer that I spent with her began with my choosing a book from her collection: the more pages, the better. At night, she and I would slip into our own twin bed in her bedroom—the only air-conditioned room in the house—and read by the headboard lamp until the middle of the night. At ninety-six, Martha still reads a book or two a week.

My partner, Kim, has given me unconditional love and encouragement. When I was laid off from my job while attending school part-time, she said, "Go full-time or you'll be in school forever." When I graduated, she said, "You have a book to write; this is no time to get a job." Kim continues to exceed my dream of a partner, making every day feel like a holiday or some special event about to happen.

My son Christo has been an inspiration. He lives the "Bypass Your Impasse" way every day—as a single parent, as a survivor of Crohn's Disease since the age of ten, and as a college student diligently working toward law school. When I'm feeling low or sluggish, I can count on Christo's quick wit and humor to get me going again.

My son Marcus is my "wonderment" child. He goes at life like there's no tomorrow—whether riding off to the mountains for the day on his motorcycle, playing a part in a movie, or crafting a song on his guitar. When he asks for my advice, he not only applies it but follows up with a text telling me how much it meant to him and that the advice really worked.

My sister, Kimberly, gave me confidence. Growing up, I studied her every move, knowing that two years later, I would be just like her. Kim has been a great role model.

My aunt, Nancy, gave me fun. She lives in perpetual motion, on the lookout for new and creative ways to enjoy life.

My father, Larry, gave me optimism and entrepreneurialism. He was the one who introduced me to the masterworks of Og Mandino, Napoleon Hill, Zig Zigler, and Dale Carnegie—words that launched my journey of always looking for the best that life has to offer.

My father's wife, Carol, has given me tenacity. Despite her own medical struggles, she regularly picks up the phone to tell me how far she rode her bike or how well her business is doing.

Text You would've remained a simple blog if not for Bill and Steve Harrison, of Bradley Communications. More than a year before I put pen to paper, I began reading every monthly newsletter they sent and listening to every interview they conducted. In this rapidly changing publishing industry, they are the pacesetters, helping aspiring authors with so much more than writing. Join them at www.FreePublicity.com if you intend to write a book.

Every author sings their editor's praises, but mine really was the best. I sent a couple of Text You messages detailing the kind of editor I wanted, with a few nonnegotiables. I posted several inquiries on Facebook to my "QL" teammates. After filtering out the referrals that didn't meet my needs, there she was: the one who fit my quest perfectly. Marj Hahne listened carefully to my vision and, through creative editing (deleting and rephrasing), delivered the book I intended to write.

There are so many others to thank who have passed through my life, and I hold them close to my heart.

OMG, She's Naked and Needs Serious Help

That was the title of a blog that raised over $1000 for the cover of *Text You*. I wanted my blog readers to be involved in the creation of this book. What an unbelievable response and experience.

After all the contributions came in, I put the sum total up for bid to cover designers around the world, through a forward-thinking design company, www.crowdSPRING.com.

Luckily, one of the stipulations was that people got to vote for the cover. I never could've chosen one of the 165 designs—smart, creative, gorgeous—on my own.

The winning cover designer:

Pure Fusion Media
www.purefusionmedia.com
4805 Marymead Drive, Fairfax, VA 22030
(615) 207-6420

Thank you to all who made those donations to "dress" Text You:

Kim Wallace	Vickie Hill
Susan Cicero	Tyler Hill
Marcus Acosta	Susan Zuppardo
Drew Sweany	Jennifer Walls
Christo Acosta	Myrna Roman
Shana McAllister	Carmen Ramirez
Camlo Acosta	Chunka Mui
Ava McAllister	Beth Mui
Drew Stiles	Bonnie Park
Nate Stiles	Jan McDade
Meadow Stiles	Stephanie Gallagher
Lily Stiles	Jack Riley Williamson
Donna Kolodziejski	Kate Riley Williamson
Tony Kolodziejski	Hannah Sparks
Nancy Eade	Louise Barma
Nelda Fuller	Louis Brisson
Vicki Morris	Phillipe Brisson
Deborah Casey	Catherine Brisson
Jonni Kennedy	Alex Brisson
Kimberly Kolodziejski	Carol Klotz
Chris Kolodziejski	Larry Klotz
Michael Kolodziejski	Mark Lares
Krystyn Kolodziejski	Marla Kennedy
Bryce Kolodziejski	Barbara Witherite
Megan Philips	Amy Witherite
Jackie Mickle	Kelly Sanders
Tammy Bailey	Lynn Heinemann
Bo Bailey	Betty Wallace
Chase Bailey	Mayor Doyle Wallace

TEXT YOU Change Your Life – One Text at a Time

Get Published

We really want to hear your Text You success story!

If you'll permit us to consider your story for publication in a new book we're creating, email it as a Microsoft Word document, including your name as you'd like it to appear, to:

Kacosta@TextYouBook.com

As a bonus, we'll send you the new e-book for free.

Thank you for being part of Text You.

Keep in touch with us by visiting:

www.TextYouBook.com

Recommended Reading

Achor, Shawn. *The Happiness Advantage: The Seven Principles of Positive Psychology That Fuel Success and Performance at Work.* Random House, 2010.

Carnegie, Dale. *How to Win Friends and Influence People.* Simon & Schuster, 1936.

Cohen, Alan. *A Deep Breath of Life: Daily Inspiration for Heart-Centered Living.* Hay House, 1996.

Ferris, Timothy. *The 4-Hour Workweek: Escape 9–5, Live Anywhere, and Join the New Rich.* Random House, 2009.

Hill, Napoleon. *Think and Grow Rich.* Fawcett Crest, 1960.

Klauser, Henriette Anne. *Write It Down, Make It Happen: Knowing What You Want—and Getting It.* Simon & Schuster, 2000.

Lipton-Dibner, Wendy. *Shatter Your Speed Limits: Fast-Track Your Success and Get What You Truly Want in Business and in Life.* Professional Impact, 2011.

Mandino, Og. *Og Mandino's University of Success.* Bantam Books, 1982.

McGinnis, Alan Loy. *Bringing Out the Best in People: How to Enjoy Helping Others Excel.* Augsburg Books, 1985.

Murphy, Joseph. *The Power of Your Subconcious Mind.* Reward Books, 2000.

Pausch, Randy. *The Last Lecture.* Hyperion, 2008.

Peale, Norman Vincent. *The Power of Positive Thinking.* Ballantine Books, 1952.

Richardson, Cheryl. *Take Time for Your Life: A 7-Step Program for Creating the Life You Want.* Random House, 1999.

Rubin, Gretchen. *The Happiness Project: Or, Why I Spent a Year Trying to Sing in the Morning, Clean My Closets, Fight Right, Read Aristotle, and Generally Have More Fun.* HarperCollins, 2009.

Schwartz, David J. *The Magic of Thinking Big.* Simon & Schuster, 1987.

Seligman, Martin E.P. *Flourish: A Visionary New Understanding of Happiness and Well-being.* Free Press, 2011.

for

Jonni Kennedy
(1965–2011)

my best friend
an angel in our midst
forever the optimist

She embodied gratitude, giving, and
living life to the fullest.
No matter the circumstances,
she was thrilled just to participate.

www.ingramcontent.com/pod-product-compliance
Lightning Source LLC
Chambersburg PA
CBHW031321040426

42443CB00005B/181